CERTAIN FIRES, CERTAIN LIGHTS:
JEREMY HILTON AT 80
Edited by Giles Goodland, Keith Jebb and David Miller

Newton-le-Willows

Published in the United Kingdom in 2025
by The Knives Forks And Spoons Press,
51 Pipit Avenue,
Newton-le-Willows,
Merseyside,
WA12 9RG.

ISBN 978-1-916590-11-3

Copyright © Giles Goodland, Keith Jebb and David Miller, 2025

Copyright for individual contributions, including quotations from Jeremy Hilton's poems © with the individual authors, 2025

Cover image (untitled ink painting by David Miller) © David Miller, 2025

Acknowledgments:

'the Southern Cross' and 'the South Alligator River' were published as *The Southern Cross*, by Jeremy Hilton, Kater Murr's Press, 2021.

Lynne Hjelmgaard's poems appeared in her book *The Turpentine Tree*, Seren, 2023.

Patricia Leighton's poem 'old man of high wood' originally appeared in *Dreamcatcher* magazine.

David Miller's poem 'Isn't or is' was first published in his chapbook *Some Other Days and Nights*, above/ground press, 2021.

The final poems in this book, by Clive Wilmer and Jeremy Hilton respectively, originally appeared on facing pages, but in reverse order, in CW's Trinity College magazine, *Pawn*.

We regret and apologise for any quotations that have not been acknowledged; we have tried our best to trace the authors, but have not always succeeded.

Contents

Preface	7
JEREMY HILTON	9
HARRY ANDERSON	11
VAL BRIDGE	12
IAN BRINTON	13
SEAN BURN	16
LESLEY BURT	17
DAVID CADDY	18
SIMON COLLINGS	22
LYNDON DAVIES	23
OWEN DAVIS	24
ANDREW DUNCAN	27
ALLEN FISHER	32
MÉLISANDE FITZSIMONS	33
JOHN FREEMAN	34
ULLI FREER	37
JESSE GLASS	39
GILES GOODLAND	40
CHRISTOPHER GUTKIND	41
JANET HANCOCK	42
GRAHAM HARTILL	44
JEFF HILSON	46
LYNNE HJELMGAARD	48
RIC HOOL	51
KEITH JEBB	52
NORMAN JOPE	53
CHRISTINE KOUTELIERI	56
PATRICIA LEIGHTON	57
RUPERT M LOYDELL	60
PHIL MAILLARD	61
CHRIS McCABE	62
DAVID MILLER	64
ESTER MUCHAWSKY-SCHNAPPER	66
JOHN MUCKLE	68

HELEN NORTHFIELD	70
CHRIS OZZARD	71
ELAINE RANDELL	74
ANTHONY RUDOLF	76
AIDAN SEMMENS	77
SAM SMITH	79
SIMON SMITH	80
STEVE SPENCE	81
PAUL SURMAN	83
MICHAEL W THOMAS	86
SCOTT THURSTON	88
CHRIS TORRANCE	89
CAROL WATTS	91
JOHN WELCH	92
CHARLES WILKINSON	94
MERRYN WILLIAMS	97
CLIVE WILMER	98
JEREMY HILTON	100

CERTAIN FIRES, CERTAIN LIGHTS:
JEREMY HILTON AT 80

Preface

When we learned that Jeremy Hilton would be eighty in February 2025, we decided that the occasion should be marked by a celebratory publication; one which would involve as many of Jeremy's fellow poets and friends as possible, and which would bear witness to his singular importance, as poet, editor, friend and more.

Some of us got to know Jeremy through his poetry, some through poetry readings and other literary events, some through his editorship of the splendid magazine *Fire*, which exemplified his generosity and his vision of poetry as something apart from "schools" or careers or dogmas, some in other ways again. As evident from the contributions in this book, we are all grateful for his presence and his activities over many decades.

The great boxing champion Sugar Ray Robinson said of one of his fellow boxers, Randolph Turpin, "As a fighter, Turpin is about one of the best I've ever met; as a gentleman, he's a wonderful fellow. Those of you who haven't had the pleasure of knowing him, Randy is one of the most regular guys you'll ever meet". If we substituted "As a poet, Jeremy's one of the best we've ever met" (and "Jeremy is one of the most regular guys"), we think that could stand as a conclusion.

JEREMY HILTON The Southern Cross

skies lower than encircling bush
        smouldering points of flame
grieve the road, graves, azure guitar
            of apostle-birds
yes there were twelve moving their
        stations, twelve arcs of torchlight
            bright amid the myriad

the driest sky, embers of the Cross
        bronze wing of the Capricorn arch
night warmth of meridian shadow
                in time with
                      tropic, trumpet

woodpecker haunts the anthills with
        harsh flute heavenwards
sun on pathways, nature's pure blue
        buzzard's far-stemming eye
the yearning for days like these
            remnant of wonder
            not yet lost

and so Centaurus' stars, luminous Canopus
        arc the clear canyon not cold
            as Daly Waters drops to dark
celestial pinpricks to speak a plains wanderer
        across moonless midnight
            Cross's sharp startle

JEREMY HILTON The South Alligator River

surges swollen through hinterland plains
cruised by crocs though none to be seen
of many rivers in the tropical Top End
all prone to flooding after wet season rains
this is the widest, most powerful, most mean
though not for marsh-birds prodding stagnant ponds
that overflowing waters have left with bounty bound

and so we spot the quiet unassuming sand-
pipers, the pelicans, ibis, egrets and spoon-
bills, and towering over all even stilts with legs clownishly long
the august black-necked Jabiru stands
of storks, of all the marsh-birds, it is king
this small patch of brackish pool its throne
while flying over making for taller sedge to land
in cover, come the cranes whose native name
is Brolga the girl whose everlasting dance
is consumed by whirling dust-storms and becomes a crane

to the east rise hills whose rocky mounds
bear outlines of beasts painted on overhangs
further beyond is Arnhem that vast tract of tribal lands
belonging to wallaby, dingo, eagle and snake
where humans tread lightly if they tread at all
and ancestral spirits pattern their dance
of earth's mad thunder whipping waters blind

while here in a swathe of seething, saltwater swirls to sea
a cruel and cloudy ocean deceptively calm
no roads or tracks will reach those shores
only this spate-prone river pulsing through these lands
of little-charted swamp and forest and only one
or two slipways for boats to leave the car
-parks to Willie Wagtail and brave the fangs
and hunger of crocodiles lurking unseen

HARRY ANDERSON From an Old Story

(For Jeremy Hilton)

Wind-flogged, buildings on fire behind them,
survivors would have to find a way to cross a watery abyss:

a monarch falling on his sword,
in anamorph.

VAL BRIDGE a stick of rock

The stick of rock chap
poet through and through
sits in the corner

orders scampi and chips, blackberry and apple crumble,
over background chitter chatter, a glow of
hockey-player faces, the smell of coffee,

he opens an estuary, fills in land to sea
wide sky over endless waves
days' shift, the tide-line

pop-popping slither of bladderwrack;
winds in and out again the taste of sea,
kri kri kri, flap-flap-flip of wings

Canada geese, a light touch calls in a skein
of v swirls, a sky shuffle of light and cloud
pterodactyls dressed as black capped gulls;

transplants oyster sheen days
a full loved wide world canvas
a quintessence of music

over scampi and chips
blackberry and apple crumble
with custard

he's a stick-of-rock chap, strengthens
compassion with a chuckle,
tends the fire

IAN BRINTON Two Pieces of Writing to Celebrate Jeremy Hilton's 80th Birthday

'Undoing distances: the permanent in the fugitive'

I.

When Eric Mottram published his seminal essay on 'The British Poetry Revival 1960-1974' in a Conference booklet for The Polytechnic of Central London he made it clear that the poem could be 'a proposition of energies which suggest their sources and do not terminate in insistent limits'. Parameters for this new poetry might include 'geology, geography, etymology and history' and they took into account the vital importance of Donald Allen's 1960 anthology of *The New American Poetry*. Given these parameters it was entirely appropriate that Jeremy Hilton's poetry should have been included in issues of *Poetry Review* during the time of Mottram's editorship and in Volume 65, Number 4 he was to contemplate music that 'led me / always on to more rainswept places / surrounded by more and / more sea, the breakers full on / rocks of barren shores'

Jeremy had contributed to an earlier issue of that groundbreaking editorship of the magazine with his opening poem from Volume 63, Number 1 in the Spring of 1972; 'Flimby pit' and his vivid realisation of a gone world of distances was to stand alongside poems by Jerome Rothenberg and Allen Ginsberg:

>   a solitary man on a vast waste
>   of slag, coal-dust
>   mine-refuse surrounding
>   the huge ramshackle
>   pit – a man
>   in black miner's
>   garb prodding with a pick
>   the expanse he
>   protrudes from, and a
>   bog-brown sack beside him

This 'lone man' seems as if he has just stepped out from years 'of bent grind' with 'mouth held tight shut' and the poet turns to 'look out the deep-hued sea' which lies on just the other side of the main road, a sea that is 'furrowed by the playful wind'.

Charles Olson had written his short poem 'These Days' back in January 1950 when Jeremy would himself have been nearly five years old and its haunting lines echo throughout the British poet's work:

> whatever you have to say, leave
> the roots on, let them
> dangle
>
> And the dirt
>
>   Just to make clear
>   where they come from

In one of Hilton's early poems published in *The English Intelligencer* where it stands alongside work by John James, Peter Riley and Jeremy Prynne, he had told us of his reading Olson's 'The Distances' whilst being on the deck of the vessel which served on the Irish Sea route between Cork and Fishguard, the Innisfallen. Voyaging on 'that old tramp hulk, black tramp, that / crowds an empty sea' he watched 'a precious / northern waters dawn' as it crept calm before bursting through as if to prompt him to wonder if 'the object' is to 'undo distance':

>   You can teach the
> Young nothing – only to know your
> brute deck, hard Innisfallen, perhaps
> how calm waves walk to
> dawn's fairness, what you give
> me, Distances, Innisfallen, your strangers flung
> on dark sea, – In Thicket – You have
> love, and no object – is the birth of water

In a letter sent to Mottram in April 1972 Hilton wrote that 'it is difficult to get down in words the joy and enthusiasm I feel over your three issues of *Poetry Review* – what a great awakening they bring'.

II. Le paysan

The farm labourer lay stretched out close beside me, eyes shut, dark eyelashes retaining their moisture – yet gently touched by light his young face seemed at peace. The strain of labour in the features relaxes at the gentle touch, his breathing soothes down and the beating heart quietens. His young chest lifts and falls with no haste now; it reveals itself, hides, and then reveals itself once more close beside the glinting gold of straw lit by a pool of sky: a tuft of cornflowers miraculously saved in the last swathe ... O my brother, your hand grasped in my own now relaxes; the heat of its blood-flow returns to its natural source. I can still feel it albeit only softly now, like a gesture of farewell recording a fading presence. You are drifting into stillness and beneath your closed eyes the life of what has passed continues to move; transparent already you are before me.

Gustave Roud from 'Requiem' translated by Ian Brinton

SEAN BURN solway firth, september 24ce

tumbril ov oystercatcher, cackle ov gull
sunsets plum tumbling from rag-cloud

leaving urologys pisstake 'but is the pain
exquisite yet?' far-behind

young couple
rev-up, jump out n to this night-bench

a final curlew pibroching
(tomorrow repeats for some)

LESLEY BURT Ruby looks for a lift

(for Jeremy Hilton, especially because it made him laugh)

Once upon a long weekend in an Airbnb cottage, Ruby becomes bored among forest brambles, berries & ferns, sick of the scrape of spoons on saucepans in the scullery, gran's demands for thin-sliced Hovis (why on earth did they have to bring her), the stink of softboiled eggs & her brother's X-Box chat (in that adolescent squeak-&-growl). Following Top Models on Instagram has immersed her in luxury brand images, heightened her passion for shopping & shoes. So, on an afternoon while her father's out chopping logs for the wood-burner, she strokes on another coat of crimson lipstick, wriggles into a skinny minidress & hauls her boots thigh-high. She'll hitch to town to look for a green-eyed man who's handsome as Micheal Ward, sounds like Richard Burton & wears Diamond Light Jimmy Choos. Oh, & she won't be back any time soon.

DAVID CADDY Jeremy Hilton

I have been blessed to have known and admired Jeremy Hilton for more than forty years. He is a great poet, novelist, prose writer, and composer of string quartets. Jeremy is an affirmative and wise man with a wide range of interests and knowledge, especially of walking, ornithology, music, sociology, social anthropology, history, geography, and the natural world.

I first saw him read in the early Eighties, alongside Paul Matthews and Owen Davis. He made an immediate impression with tightly woven, observational poems read in a clear and authoritative manner. His poetry, full of precise and poignant detail, is acutely socially aware with a deep affinity towards the outsider and the world of living things. His generosity of spirit and enthusiasm for a wide variety of poetry and poetics is well known. He has travelled widely to support friends, poets, and organisers at events up and down the country for decades. He is, in short, the epitome of a genuine poetry enthusiast who has brilliantly served the wider poetry community by his presence. He is a treasure and deserves to be celebrated for all that he has contributed to the poetry world.

Jeremy was a fine editor of *FIRE* magazine from 1995 to 2012 with the strength of his convictions never being swayed by reputation or non-literary matters. His catholic and internationalist taste tolerated both the experimental and traditional as well as translations. He also pointedly encouraged young poets and was happy to favour the raw over the cooked. Each substantial issue was a delight to hold and read.

Jeremy's deep concern for the young stems from his career as a social worker and his deep awareness and knowledge of the emotional damage of social deprivation, especially on children. His poetry is sensitive to the emotional lives and losses of children. This enters at the level of ordinary experience shifting between inner and outer lives and manages to avoid binary thinking by going from the localised to the global and universal. It is this wide-eyed focus that serves to elevate his poetry. Jeremy's direct speech approach stems from wide ranging reading, especially of William Carlos Williams, the Beats, Charles Olson, Robert Duncan, Basil Bunting, and Gael Turnbull, who was a close friend, amongst many others.

Jeremy has been a long-standing supporter of *Tears in the Fence* magazine, its series of festivals and workshops since the late eighties. He has been a popular contributor of poetry, reviews, and essays to the journal for decades. As a stalwart of the *Tears in the Fence* White Horse workshop for the past eight years, his presence is a joy to everyone present. His contributions to the critical section of the workshop have revealed a poet, who was fully formed at a young age and has continued to produce timeless poetry since the late sixties. The workshop group has been privileged to follow and comment upon the emergence of two extraordinary books, which dovetail well together. *Fulmar's Wing* (KFS Press, 2022), a 75-poem sequence of irregular sonnets on the climate and migration crises and *Far World From Silesia* (Brimstone Press, 2022), a collection inspired by the nineteenth century explorer, Emin Pasha's life in Central Africa in the 1880s.

Historical, geographical, sociological and meteorological conditions and forces weave through both books alongside an enormous range of birds and animals. Birdwatching is one of Jeremy's favourite interests and it is the act of patient observation and an appreciation of the wider world that hits the reader and listener when encountering his poems as sonic movements.

25

a rainy mist, a grainy light not quite
                        darkness or light
     shrouding the everywhere
birds gearing up for nest-time for sex
chasing spectres or each other, herring
                      -gulls on roof ridges
    magpies into the tallest tree
blackbirds but both are males! – across

and:

26

20 giraffes tall in a truck ferried in groups of
              seven across the river Nile
two wheatears rest on a lonely hilltop
a crossroads appears twice in the mythical mind
                      waterlogged ground drying
fulmars gliding grey, straight-winged – water
                  that doesn't change, oil
discoveries threatening traditional habitats of
                giraffes in Uganda, ground

Fulmar's Wing has been justly recognised as an exceptional and timely book and deserves all the accolades that it receives. *Far World From Silesia* is a hybrid work combining poetry, prose and essay exploring the life and works of Emin Pasha. The parallel texts across each page combine historical, geographical and natural history insights. Pasha collected some 2600 species, including notable birds, flora, fauna, insects and other creatures found in Central Africa. His poems capture the horrors of the Congo Free State, which 'was / never free, its mineral wealth transposed / to an iron fist, its wide waterway where the hippos wallowed / starts to be scarred by the hulks of abandoned ships / and stained by the blood seeping from banks and slopes.'

To be as universally admired and respected as Jeremy is both a tremendous achievement and something that more poets should aspire towards. Jeremy is, above all, a giver and offers his enthusiasms and support unconditionally. He is neither a player nor a user at a time when poetry has too many such figures. In consequence, Jeremy is less well known as a poet and not recognised as the distinguished poet that his friends and others know him to be. Jeremy is a blessing and a man to treasure.

DAVID CADDY The Bamboo Bridge

(For Jeremy Hilton)

Water drips from a red clay pipe, the drinking well has no bucket. There's a shiny standpipe outside the thatch cottage and beside a sense of springs and high water table the brook flows fast. Small ash, alder trees cover well-trodden steps to the sandstone bed. There are fish aplenty in 1961. Downstream by May Cottage the wobbly bamboo bridge tied with hemp and lashing cord, rickety, but with enough give to prevent toppling, was stronger in my mind than the wooden shed built around the oak on the other side. I always lingered and took the breeze before walking to the stone bridge, where I blocked the ditch and got wet with the joy of playing with mud and wood. My grandfather repaired and built bridges after the War. He had laid and blown-up bridges around Arnhem and Nijmegen, and taught my father the art of beam and girder. After the War, men were called hands. I never had to use my hands, maybe a ball of cork and string, some primordial urge to strike, pull and drive for no obvious purpose beyond the sheer pleasure of doing so. Thumped, not rule of thumb. Moist sods. That piece of heaven over the brook built by the dexterity of a tenant smallholder, testimony to his aspirations and experiences overseas.

SIMON COLLINGS A Visit to a Poet

(For Jeremy Hilton)

I was travelling by train to visit a poet friend who lived on the coast in a rural part of the country. There were only two other passengers in the single carriage by the time we neared the end of the line. From overheard snatches of their conversation they appeared to be bird watchers. I had been re-reading some of my friend's poems and when we approached the station I took off my reading glasses. As I did so the ends of both arms shattered into fragments in my hands. The train was slowing to a stop, so I pushed the broken spectacles into my shirt pocket and began to gather my possessions. There was a pile of litter on the floor, which I recognised as mine, though I was surprised to see it there. I picked up as much of it as I could manage and followed my fellow passengers off the train. They were discussing sea birds. On the platform I looked around for a bin. A large black container stood nearby, full of garden waste. I noticed another further along which was packed with hedge trimmings. The station looked overgrown and neglected. The train had pulled away into a siding and on the tracks a man in overalls was busy uprooting thistles. I made my way to the exit, passing a mass of flowering ivy on which a host of red admirals were feeding. Jeremy was waiting for me at the exit. His spectacles, I noticed, were held together with duct tape.

LYNDON DAVIES Response

(For Jeremy Hilton)

Mistle thrush on its lit wall:
all listening, but then that twitch
into call.

A trill throbs
in the open, asserts its hollow.

Surprised by cadenza
as if suddenly finding itself piqued
to resume to consolidate.

So full of its own space,
the urge and the means given,
just getting on with it. I wonder
where all the mute ones are?

You can't tell by looking,
but maybe even the afflicted
are lulled held by that flung voice,
soaring out through the light's

late dazzling flourish. Can we say
we have heard? can we recognize
what was said

is said is saying still?

OWEN DAVIS The Last Visitor

(for Jeremy)

Do you pause
Where Truth lies
Bleeding?

Or at the place
Beauty was shot
Stone dead?

Between them,
Is only the width
Of an envelope.

You know that.
But it surprised
God, so I hear.

He knows so little, doesn't He.
Listen, then.
Only if you wish to:

By a way, not
On any map,
Seldom trod,

Is a village.
Of hearts unbroken.
You'd like it there.

The trees have many hands
To feel the sky with.
They have bones that sigh.

In that sense,
They're people, like us.
Born without hope,

That learn, at the end,
To hope with a fury,
As darkness wraps them up.

The scent of wood smoke
Lives everywhere.
Thatch and cobbles and plum trees,

All of them, send out messages
Made from it.
Blue sentences, you might say,

Rising in plumes from every home
Into clear midwinter skies.
Telling the tale, but I'm guessing,

Of how breath once met the breathless
And made the first frightened man.
Who kept a robin on his finger, so it's told.

Offering it Poetry.
Until it languished
From hunger, and then died.

A long sound, too.
Can you hear it?
The deaf can.

A river, perhaps?
Both friend and enemy.
Bringing down the silver fishes.

Taking away the child.
For his splendid curiosity,
He's wrapped in weeds now

And cannot ever dream again.
Arguing into the distance
About the colour of angels,

The river can't be sorry,
Though surely it would try.
Oh, but it knows why the kingfisher's

Sharp kiss hurts like it does.
Why the swans, always, will turn
Their fierce and lovely backs against you.

No, that was it.
Not a river.
I remember now.

Conversation!
The longest sound of all.
Humans everywhere are made from it.

Words, yes, then no words.
And both are suitable.
I reached that village,

Once, and all alone.
It was a mistake.
Or, so I thought.

Because I was young,
I left, within the hour.
Because of love!

Yes, that was it.
I had tears still in me.
I had friends to meet.

And myself.
And something beyond us both.
A village of hearts unbroken?

It's all yours.
Go on, look at a map.
Choose any path you like.

Be the final visitor.

ANDREW DUNCAN Jeremy Hilton and *Fire*

(For Jeremy Hilton)

I acquired all the volumes of Jeremy Hilton's magazine *Fire* as they came out, between 1994 and 2012, and caught up with the ones I hadn't read when I retired in 2018. 35 issues. So 4000 pages altogether? Is that right? A bit less maybe? I am looking at the back cover of #28, 2007, and can see that it lists 123 poets included inside the issue.

I think the most vital feature of *Fire* was its wide-spectrum approach, and to get with that we have to return to the situation of the 1990s. This was summed up in two series of talks in Exeter under the rubric "Binary Myths" (in roughly 1997 and 1998, and published in two volumes under the same title): the idea was that the poetry world was split. People crudely divided the poetry world into two parts, the part which likes me and the part which doesn't. And that individuals seldom read anything outside the area which they, factionally, identified with. This was worse for people who had been polarised for 30 years than for people who had only suffered from it for, say, five years. A corollary is the suggestion that constantly following habits in choosing what to read may lead to a trap, a box in which the most pleasurable sensations are to be found by challenging your own orthodoxies. If you have spent 30 years ignoring mainstream poetry, it is likely that the most exciting poetry that you aren't aware of is hidden within that negation. You will find it by discarding your selectivity – a block of preferences which was once an asset and has become a dogma. People were *determined* to avoid what they disliked. Their views dated back, in some cases, to the early 1970s, and were not being updated. They did not know that the mainstream had changed between, say, 1974 and 1995. On the other side, people never encountered anything Alternative, and did not even know what the alternative of the 1970s had stood for. They did not necessarily know that it existed. In selecting, people saw merely surface features of a poet's work and immediately switched off: they felt they were simply in the wrong place. Such "no, I don't listen to jazz" reactions were quite different from rounded reactions to a book as a whole.

So, everyone stood to benefit from breaking down a few barriers. In the talks series, people seemed to grasp depolarisation as meaning *everyone who disagrees with me should vanish,* and *everyone who doesn't like my poetry is suffering from a terrible illusion.* Nobody offered to change their own behaviour. Obviously, if nobody moves an inch, then the whole scene will not move an inch, and polarisation itself will not shift. So the talkers hadn't really grasped the project.

Fire was part of a genuine depolarisation project; it put its money where its mouth was by attracting and accepting poems from a very wide spectrum. Simply by reading it, you were going outside the sacred precincts of the Avant Garde.

In 1966, a group of poets recognised that English poetry was so bad that it was in danger of dying out. This situation was made acute by the presence of American poetry, visibly capable of taking over the market. The solution proposed was to have a group learning project, where thoughtful poets would read and criticise each other's work and would eventually become, not just the primary readers, but the primary writers, for each other. They communicated via a mailed-out newsletter called *The English Intelligencer*. One of the participants was Jeremy Hilton. In 1974, Eric Mottram listed him as one of the vital poets of the British Poetry Revival, in his exhibition at the Polytechnic of Central London. His name crops up again, this time as a guest editor, developing a special 1975 issue (#11) of *Joe Di Maggio* which was an anthology of poems about place. This was, obviously, related to the TEI project, which had found geography and deep time as its special interests. (This was, also, a way of uncovering the English peculiarities which were, at first glance, the reasons for failure to compete with the Americans.) Eric Mottram's second exhibition at the Polytechnic of Central London, in 1977, with its theme of geography, seems to have drawn lavishly on Hilton's definition of the area. This recital serves also to show that Hilton was someone who did shift his own centre, to enter the new depolarised space: he had to leave behind the avant garde comfort zone.

Hilton wrote sparse editorials, but issue 18, 2002, has what looks like a follow-up to the Place issue of *Joe Di Maggio*, in 1975. He says, "It might seem that many of the poems and prose pieces in this issue are concerned with a sense of place, or possibly in some sense with 'nature', and there is a degree of truth in this." This is rather hesitant. But he goes on: "However, what really hangs, most, if not all, of these works together is something altogether more difficult to define, it may be seen as an absence, a silence, a darkness, 'the blank ... screen of the soul', to quote A.C. Evans. It may be seen as an underside, or shadow side, to our lives. It may perhaps pertain to night, or the moon, or to death, or to what remains unsaid. However it may be [...] described, I believe it pervades the works chosen here. What is more, I believe that this quality is something close to what may be considered to distinguish real poetry from other writing[.]". (Evans is a Gothic or Symbolist writer who wrote 'Pale angel Aemyrge', *aemyrge* is the oldest form of *embers*.) At p.141 Evans writes "I prefer deserted, empty places: negative spaces where/ I take the words I write and chant them in the Void, / This blank cinema screen of my soul" ('Maybe this is why'). This may be a hasty reaction, but this blankness sounds like space itself, as something fundamentally non-human, which swallows up human wishes, which carries distance and separation. And that may be a glimpse of *Fire*'s mission; we vanish into private and fragmented spaces because they are protective, but *Fire* was there to make public space inviting, to draw us into *other* poetic styles. To invest in each other.

In 1994, Alternative poetry was under pressure and belonged to a community which had bonded under pressure. It had come into being from a rejection, although what had been rejected was sinking increasingly into the past. But it was in danger of ignoring empty and available space opening up all around it. Its signs were soaked with loyalty, but that might imply that you had the same pattern of reactions in every poem, and new signs weren't equally interesting. It was pervaded by loyalty tests. The loyalty group aspect was oriented towards the past and discouraged experiment. Often, the scene was academic and preoccupied by classics from a generation or two in the past.

I thought to pick a few poems out of *Fire* #28, which collects poems about visual art. So, Chris Brownsword wrote:

> images lay like a torsion balance in-between these net / -works of the phone poles. Error margin squeezes down / to pinhole/measures the requirements of a larynx when / forming the tentative nouns of a psalm, washed amongst / the sodium/ potassium and chloride.
>
> (from 'Teething hydra')

Chloë Meakin wrote:

> You are the stars of dust, caught in sunlight, floating, lulling. / You are the soft blah of the pushing wind against the window frames, / the murmur of the dust mites eating up my carpet. / You are the light switches, clicking up and down at night and morning. / You are my white breath, confessing to the teacups.
>
> (from 'Lost Past Episode')

and Patrick Gasperini wrote:

> I only earn a few francs a month, though I am happy among shelves and spiders / (Mr Lunganotti ever so proud of me!): / I always fly in my robe of sea-flowers. //

> Mr Lunganotti was a water-melon, glassy and porous, / His bow tie was a red louse on the white continent of his shirt, / His trousers contained the entire Amazonian jungle.
>
> (from 'Journal of a metaphysical mutation')

Gasperini was writing modernism, but distinctly in the style of the 1920s, or so it always seemed to me. The male lead seems to be channelling Akim Tamiroff. This long poem ran over several issues. Richard Alan Bunch's poem about the colour green is theoretical and comes in blips:

> 9. Green's pigment mirrors blue's sky, returns its hues within the dissolution of time.
>
> 10. Prophetic traits realise adversity is expensive; green's darkest light creates anterior to truth alloyed.
>
> 11. What is praised are the autobiographies of green, hexagons of the dreaming self.
>
> 12. History living draws anatomy's lesson; green's peace is scaled by the heart. Red's yellow wars to be
>
> (from 'Green')

Does this give an impression of *Fire?* That is hard to assert, given how much poetry they published. How many poets? maybe 1000? it is hard to count. Hilton must have been completely committed to it, over a fifteen-year period. These are poems I would not otherwise have seen.

During the 1990s, the mainstream scene underwent a thorough renewal. Dislike of the older mainstream (the generation born in the 1920s, who had bought into the Cold War in a big way) was widespread, and obviously was a re-run of the breakaway reaction which had given rise to the Underground. The Underground was so invisible, by 1990, that a new generation of poets bypassed it altogether and wished to enter the central, public space instead. That central space failed to resist, partly for political reasons and partly because the new poets were so numerous (and talented). Hilton perceived this change and was in a position to exploit it, getting his readers used to the idea that the Seventies split was over and that there was a new landscape which had many more significant players. Hilton proposes that we emerge from our separate subspaces, and their conditional isolation. He suggests that we spend much of our time in uncertainty and hope, not protected from the unfamiliar by stylistic prejudices. He proposes, I should think, that we are here to offer comfort and company to each other. This is a description of what language does.

In the 1970s, Jeremy was writing poetry about space and place. It displaced the ego from central place. It recognised that space inherently has no centre: things like perspective derive from the insertion of a human observer into a space which itself is continuous and without high points. So this is not wholly different from the *Fire* project of depolarising cultural space.

ALLEN FISHER Farm grass, for Jeremy Hilton

You can hardly walk out
without your welded boots
occasionally headless
last heard as you hummed it
you wear your college hat lightly
in light as you glow with enthusiasm
barley and sometimes lupins,
undersown with mixtures of red and white
clover,
various grasses and herbs,
and deep-rooting lucerne.

not trapped by this moment
momentum takes you into a larger field
where you are blinded by choices
voices you continue to hear reverberate
perennial grass, clover and herbs underneath
take over
lucerne protein
deep roots access moisture and nutrients particularly
potassium great for soil structure, breaking
through layers of compaction
aiding aeration and drainage.

there is love not immediacy
meditated care in your activity
indoors vividly aware of what you reach for
in the exact moment before susurration
expands into effulgence
instead of hay-making
lactic acid, pickled silage

MÉLISANDE FITZSIMONS Jeremy

in front of me
his back shaking with
the mirth of words
his hair aflame

in his lopsided delight he reads Kim's lines
with a smile
holding her
bird of hope in the right hand

the electricity of grief live
haloed around you
un pas seul that step-on-your-own
as we switch power on in that hug

you are not always alone
Jeremy
even if sometimes
it seems easier to talk or write
from a distance

JOHN FREEMAN Fire in the Malverns

It was the evening of the summer solstice.
With three friends I had walked up from the station
into the Malvern Hills – we'd had directions,
but it amazes me that we could follow them
well enough to get where we were going.
We must have had the last glimmers of daylight.
Excitement had us talking to each other,
and our voices carried in the still night air
until we shut them off at once like motors
intruding on the silence, when we crested
a rise and saw in the hollow below us
a blazing wood fire with a group of people
round it, motionless, attentive, listening,
while one frail voice, with musical inflection,
recited what was clearly poetry.

As quietly and unobtrusively
as we could we found places to sit down,
our arrival eased by the slight let-up
in tension as the reading, after clapping,
and a short pause, was followed by somebody
telling us the name of the next reader.

Like everyone else, we were mesmerised
by the half-sung words, the night, the fire, the hills,
taking part in something archetypal.
Chris Torrance read a poem about firelight,
'the most ancient strobe of man,' he called it,
and another about the solstice, starting
'Now sol steadies,' with his gift for making
the Latin word at the heart of our word
a natural part of English, and so making
the persona of the sun more vivid to us.

I took my turn at reading with the rest.
Gael Turnbull read his poem starting
'How many miles to Babylon?/Three score

and ten,' and ending 'But I want to know
what I'm in for!/You'll not get to Babylon
then.' And he read 'You Should Have Been There,'
the speaker laughing at his memories
of a riotous social gathering,
telling something of it, hinting at more,
teasing his imagined listener, and by
extension us, hearing him repeating
from time to time, 'you, you should have been there.'
Too bad we hadn't been, but we were here now.

As the readings wound down, and the fire
burned low, we curled up in sleeping bags –
my own wasn't warm enough and I froze,
but hardly cared – dozed fitfully, and woke
to see in the dawn light wild roses near us,
their delicate white petals edged with colour.

It was Jeremy who had gathered us,
whose own poems are bedded in the wild.
He had other people working with him,
he was always good at that, but Jeremy
was the prime mover then, and later,
at a daylight festival in Malvern
where I read with, among many others,
Omar Pound, Lee Harwood and Roy Fisher.

Later still, at Chapter Arts Centre
in Cardiff – I doubt if anyone ever
put in more miles to be present at readings
and festivals – Jeremy told me he was
going to start his own magazine, and asked,
would I subscribe? Of course, I said I would,
and later sent him poems he accepted.
Whenever the next issue of it arrived,
crowded with names I knew, and more I didn't,
catholic and adventurous in its range,
it brought with it flickering memories
of clear voices reading one by one under
the stars to forty or fifty people,

listening with palpable intensity
of attention, inspired by the occasion.
In the firelight we saw each other's faces,
and whoever was standing and performing.

Experiences like this may have been
commonplace for some: for me it was unique.
A perfect fusion of natural magic
with the solitude and sharing, yin and yang,
of what a poetry community
can be at its best. I owe Jeremy
more than I can say, as many of us do,
I know, but at the heart of it for me,
and at my own heart while I live, I treasure
the event that gave his magazine its name,
when we gathered in the Malverns round a fire
at the solstice. You, you should have been there.

We were young, didn't know what we were in for.
Is it Babylon we've got to, Jeremy?

ULLI FREER For Jeremy

windswept then calm
with falling feathers as connection
messages from plants
animals and mountains carry
and embody revelation
walk off path
climb over leaning fence
go through kiss gate
to hole in rock as a mount
to ride to the upper world
of spirits or through its hole
to descend into netherworlds
to catch spirits
in the past
abundance of slate
quarried now neglected
under a tiled sky
of dense cloud
carrion crows perch
on barbed wire fence
as lookouts and cry
a song for a lamb
that they should peck
out their eyes
clutch crystals
to penetrate the opacity
of time in the highlands
between gorse thorns
strands of caught wool
with much bracken
above knee height
when one of many sheep
by the mountain gate
came through with us
though who led the way
we now cannot say
on our way lost foothills

to small lake
of jade colour
water below cwm
up scree slope accumulations
small pieces of loose
broken rock debris
below and on mountainside
small pieces of debris
loose below and on
broken rock mountainsides
in mist maybe a summit
scree our feet drum upon
now in trance state
become formed rockfalls
between natural freeze and thaw cycles

JESSE GLASS Stranded

moth (child's splay
hands wide) —
nightflower eyes staring
into emptiness

(quanta / sift / heat
10 / o'clock / gutter)

antennae
sag from
riot-helmet head

Wings
(tans, ox-bloods, muddled at the curve
pooled in whorls, lozenges of chestnut
sutured ::: golden threads :::) —

flail dust at once
clawed / tufted feet

to rise
among park pines /

d,a,r,k,l,y
a,c,t,i,v,e

beneath a wing
glimpse
Wolf Wasp
clutch moth's gilled belly applying

KEY TO THE KINGDOM
Kingdom-Come

King Nothing Comes. Wings
cool into petals of a flower.
A dog barks.

GILES GOODLAND Hell Lane

There's a path from the village. I just have to walk straight up, but I see there's a side track leading to a prominent conical hill which I had seen earlier from Jeremy's window. There is a good view from the top. Something about seeing the path ahead – your immediate future made visible through flocks of sheep, then back to what I assume is Hell Lane, but when I walk down, it doesn't seem so familiar. Feeling slightly puzzled I turn back and go up. I'm not sure that this is Hell Lane and zoom in closely on the OS app. The name comes up, so I keep on walking upwards. Yes the lane is sunken again, but I'm puzzled because this is the way I walked down. When I get to the crossroads at the top Hell Lane continues towards the village. Now this is where the Lane gets most dramatic, most sunken, most full of carvings and vegetation so deep down, the fallen trees form a bridge above me.

On the drive back, I decided to stop off at a place called Hellstone, about 10 miles along the coast eastwards, and I thought, maybe there's a connection between Hell Lane and Hellstone. The hills became steep, and the road very narrow, and then "You have arrived at your destination", but I hadn't. I was on a narrow stretch of road, so drove on to find a place to park, turning into a modern housing estate, then checking my phone and saw another turn off further on. I found that I was on an open hillside and walked up. This was private land, donkeys in paddocks, fields of cabbages, barbed wire, and then walking northwards finding huge obtund stones, part of another prehistoric constellation, and on the hilltop, there was the Dolmen, five capped stones, with the Hardy monument in the distance.

Looking back, the conical hill. Hedge against dust.

CHRISTOPHER GUTKIND Frizzing

Trees without our words,
water without our sounds,
skies without our reach,
stars without our awareness,
people with our attention,
conversations through natures,
the island without silences,
our silences in our islands.

JANET HANCOCK The Plantswoman's Tale

(For Jeremy)

They forecast frost last night
in September?
not unknown   nor in any month
they
who are expected to know
they're usually right   although
remember '87
seven oaks reduced to one

September frost does not discomfort me
my crops have had their span
yet cling on to brown saturated stalks
beneath brittle yellowing leaves
under next door's honeysuckle overhang
tomato trusses shelter
ripen still in mellow sunlight
a few beans hide among outsized dying foliage
two cucumbers assert themselves
dangle and wait for me
defy wind   rain

May is another matter
bank holiday   even Easter   weekends
I smile at garden centres
that entice spring-longing erstwhile cultivators
to buy trays of tender shoots
which will be planted out straightaway
job done   back to work next day

I delay through the third week
nurture plants in the kitchen
how much is just enough water
I ought to know by now
they're getting leggy
should have bigger pots
until afternoon's fecund warmth and promise
come on let them thrive outside

surely no more frost
each morning   how are you
you're faring well
stand up straight   we don't do wilting here
time for longer stakes

established
do they need me

there was no frost last night

GRAHAM HARTILL After Lu Ji

(For Jeremy)

1

The poet stands at the centre
   in order to deeply observe the world,
cultivating heart and mind
     by way of the ancient canon.

Through Autumn, Winter, Spring and Summer
   he sings the passage of time.
Contemplating the ten thousand things,
     she lets her thought go free.

She grieves for leaves in the burning Autumn,
   delights in the twigs of fragrant Spring.
His heart, solemn and grave, embraces frost
     but his mind towers, and overlooks clouds!

2

At first, the sunken word is unwilling to rise
   like a trout that has swallowed the hook.
Then, slowly, a phrase may flutter down
     like a feather, shed by a bright crane on her journey south.

He inquires of all that possesses a shadow,
   plays each instrument that holds a sound.
Sometimes she is a shifting tiger, outwitting all others,
     sometimes a bursting dragon, making the ducks to scatter!

The principle, in supporting the substance,
   enables the tree to stand upright.
Its patterns of hanging, reaching, boughs
     yield plentiful fruit.

When jade-stone is hidden in rocks, the mountain glimmers;
    when a pearl is enfolded by water, the river has Charm.
There's no need to hack down thorn-trees!
        Their allure is very well known by the nesting kingfisher.

3

No, let nourishing moisture given to us by cloud and rain
        and the transformations of ghost and spirit
    inscribed on metal, stone or paper
be virtues made to extend both far and wide,
    flowing through pipes and flying from strings

        and every day reviving the world!

(Lu Ji (261-303)

JEFF HILSON Wellmeadowsign 1 & 2

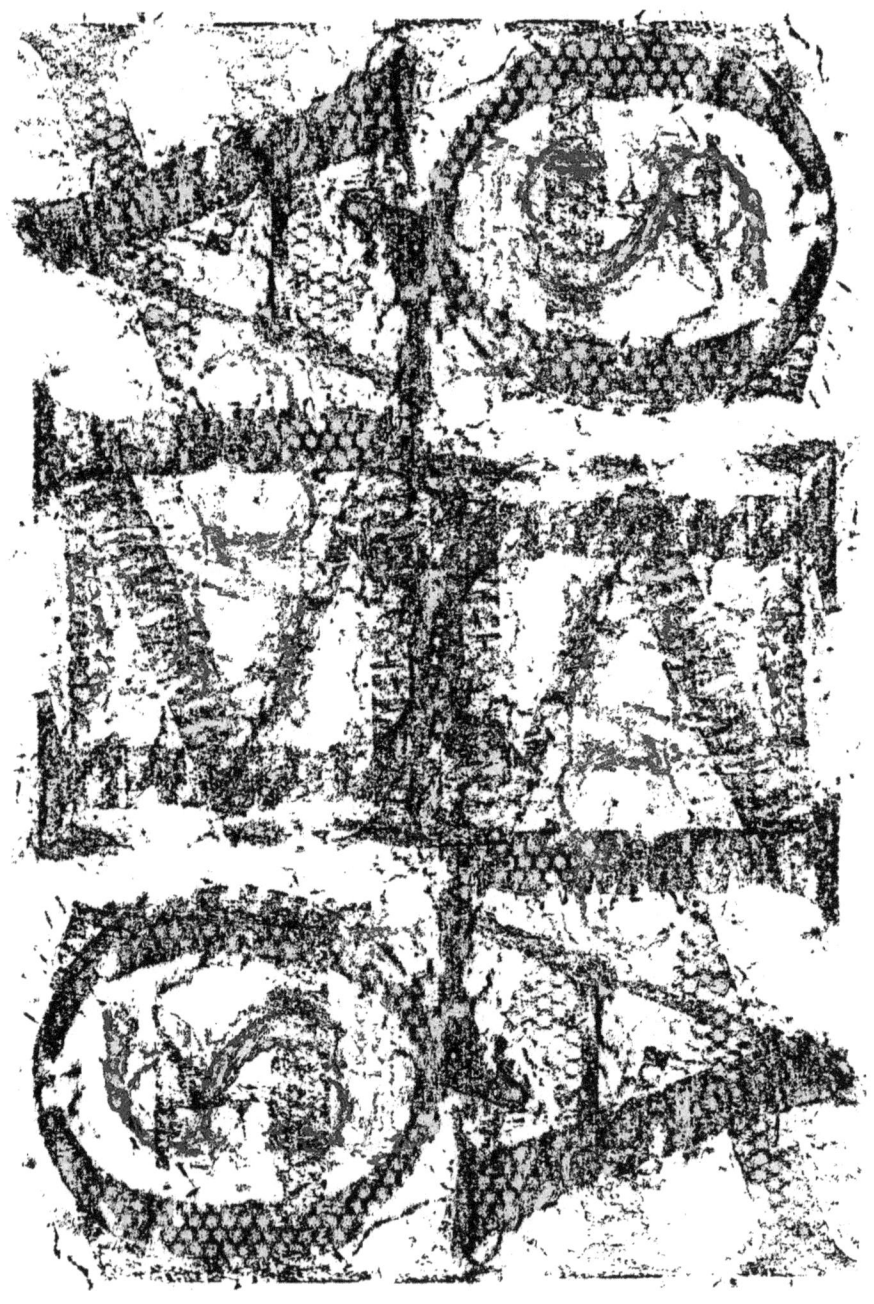

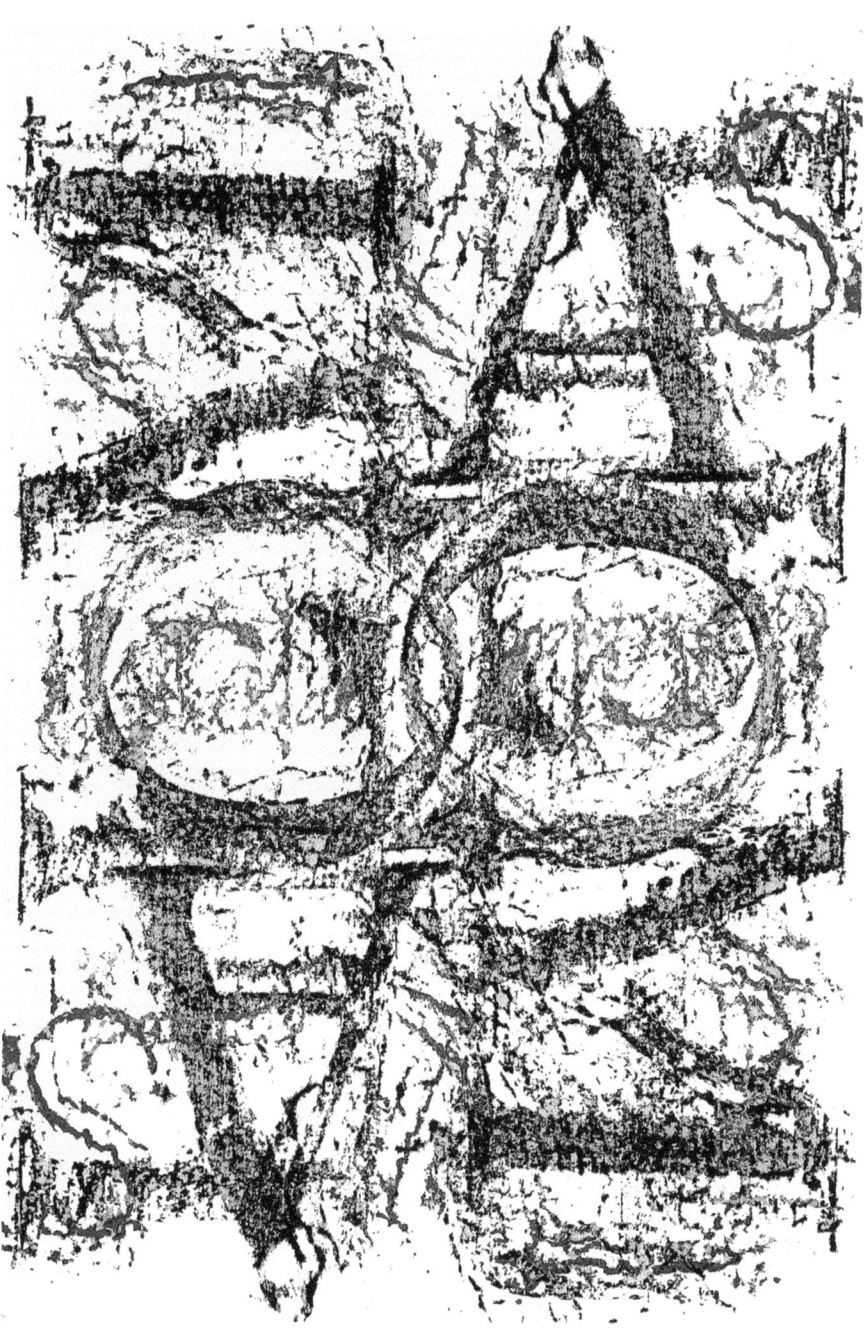

LYNNE HJELMGAARD Absence

(For Jeremy Hilton)

They deepen the world –
        lifelong friends

or friends who haven't been
        together for some time.

When we finally meet
        we can still laugh

at a familiar story
        or gesture

and between us know
        what's being thought, not said.

Do we seek
        our younger selves

inside each other,
        the person no longer here?

Many have left us now
        but absence rearranges itself

like water, like light.

LYNNE HJELMGAARD Honey

(For Jeremy Hilton)

When my fingers slide over
a sticky spot on the kitchen counter
the memory returns –

of heating milk,
of groping for honey
in the dark.

A search for sweetness
and comfort
to quiet the night's disturbance –

travelling in a dream from one airport to another,
separation from my loved one.
Where were we going that seemed so important at the time?

Now the dream is lost,
and so is the loved one –
thick and cloudy

honey in a jar
needs warmth and attention.
Before it once again can become smooth,

before it loosens
onto the spoon
and runs free.

LYNNE HJELMGAARD A Love Affair Between a Border Collie and a Wire-haired Sausage Pup on a Small Building Site

She brings him bits of an already chewed-upon
plastic bucket or what looks like
a petrified twig. He can't wait to greet her,
doing a kind of Don Juan leap and jump.
When most feverish, this hairy little bearded body
covered in wood chips and dust
searches the grounds for whatever she can find
to please him. He receives the smallest of treasures
with great delight. Sometimes, so involved with
her digging, she forgets him, though any bark,
whimper, or sideways glance in his direction
is not lost. He waits loyally, patiently.
The truest connection. Anything can happen
with such affection in the air.

RIC HOOL Wing Commander

(For Jeremy Hilton)

If poem miles were Air Miles
you'd be twice round the planet
and halfway to Mars
And when not sharing your thoughts
you are the welcome face in the audience
A paladin of the reading circuit

Wing and feather catch your eye
that airspace of movement
alerts transposition
from sky to page, taking
cadences of flight and song
that alight in words to rest
high as fulmars float on water

An Imbolc birth you arrived
with the coming of light,
Candlemass and Brigid's celebration,
the cloth of poetry about you
its making rich in pattern
taut in weave

KEITH JEBB West Bay

(For Jeremy Hilton)

roughly folded clothes   here   covered in sand
when tide and light   align   with the radio times
you will see   perrin's head   bobbing the surf

how lee harwood   saw it   from the car park
before the harbour   moved   as it does
ropes pulling the walls   west   270 yards

boulders piled   against   longshore drift
against   the seawall   catch bleached
boughs   the light   granite and spume

you want it   rougher   the sea
light shears   salts wounds   you
lear in it   when no one   with no

one about to change   sea and   sea wall
grey hairs in   green wrack   west bay cliffs
ochre stone   looms   west of what?

1.11.2024

NORMAN JOPE Jeremy Hilton at 80 – Keeping the World in Mind

It was in the early 1990s when I first became aware of Jeremy Hilton's work, initially via our mutual friendship with Tim Allen, and I've been impressed from the outset. Jeremy has gone on to publish a considerable quantity of my own writing in his magazine *Fire*, as well as reviewing one of my collections in *Tears in the Fence*, and I was pleased to return the favour – up to a point – by facilitating the publication of his chapbook *Earth Bound* by Phlebas Press (the small press imprint of my late friend Roderick Muncey) in 2000.

We would have met for the first time during that period, and in particular I recall a visit I made to Jeremy and Kim in Malvern in 1998 and a walk on Worcestershire Beacon. Since then, we've met occasionally – most recently at the two most recent Tears in the Fence Festivals – and, when I read at Ric Hool's Hen and Chicks event in 2019, in Abergavenny, it was an honour and a surprise that he had driven all the way from Bridport for the reading. That is a round trip of around 250 miles.

Most of my poetry collection is in storage – it doesn't now look as though the book-lined study I promised myself will ever materialise – so, in writing this tribute, I'm going to confine myself to Jeremy's recent KFS collection *Fulmar's Wing*. It's an excellent introduction to his work, bringing together his key themes, and the ambition and range of this sequence is characteristic of his oeuvre.

If there's one thing that I value most in his poetry, then perhaps it's the global reach of it. Opening the book at random, I go from Lancashire to Uganda: from Zanzibar to the Oxus (in Central Asia): from Guatemala to Sri Lanka: and from Cox's Bazar (in Bangladesh) to Damascus. This is suggestive of the visionary geography of Hölderlin's late poems, although in Jeremy's case there is a more rational organising presence. What he does – and perhaps this isn't as commonplace as one might have expected in 2024 – is to write as a genuine citizen of the world (or a 'citizen of nowhere' in ignorantly nativist terms), and he does so with a depth of compassion that matches his technical skill.

A key theme of the book is the experience of refugees, the 'already-robbed of this world' (Section 6), the number of which is only likely to increase in response to climate change and conflict. In 2015, I encountered the mainly-Syrian refugees massed in the underpasses at Budapest's Keleti station – brought there as if as unwitting extras in a propaganda film, allegedly staged by the Hungarian government to illustrate the threat of 'illegal migration' to its electorate – and a few days later, back in Plymouth, I watched the news footage of their march out of Budapest, down familiar streets and onto the motorway to Vienna. When we come to see our fellow humans as a problem, then all kinds of abuse become permissible and we are all trapped behind 'borders of hard-wire and high cameras' (Section 29).

The sequence, taken as a whole, is a mental map of our contemporary reality in which the (generally involuntary) movements of human beings across the globe, whether for political reasons or in response to climate change, is compared to and contrasted with the natural migration patterns of (mainly) birds. Jeremy is a keen and highly knowledgeable ornithologist, and this collection is as rich in reference to the world of birds – and indeed the rich scenery of his adopted Dorset - as it is to the (equally precarious) world of humans in the 21st century. It is a world in which (Section 27), 'the seabird's cry comes from the beginning of the world' and in which (Section 63) 'a whole burst of sky in the breeze/reveals sunlit hills of Dorset in the west/and lines of greening shingle'.

As such, I'm reminded that the Hungarian word for map – *térkép* – is a compound word that literally means 'space-picture'. This is a sequence of poem-maps, which present an intuitively accurate and compelling space-picture of the precarious world we inhabit, and their geographical scope is entirely equal to this task.

There might also be something even deeper at stake, which is to do with the all-too human attempt to imagine what the world might be like – for better or for worse – when we are gone. Perhaps this becomes a more urgent task for us as we grow older – when we're in our twenties and thirties, we might be relatively confident that we will still be around in fifty years' time and can therefore wait and see how things will turn out. As we grow older, the chances of our being around will inevitably diminish – and this collection, the product of age and experience, appears to seek to intuit a world that is coming into existence but of which the author will have no personal knowledge.

The fact that we *won't* know makes us all the more curious. It's by no means a comforting vision that Jeremy presents – above all, given the likely effects of climate change in terms of our 'sleepwalking off/the cliff of survival' (Section 69) – but it's a dynamic one that encourages resistance. If the present reality is one in which 'the further heat of delusion/persists, the poison promise/of wealth for all' (Section 55), then that doesn't mean that all hope is lost. Indeed, *Fulmar's Wing* could be read as a work of prophecy in the Biblical sense – rather than in the sense of unthinking clairvoyancy – charting the world-out-of-kilter that we already inhabit, and that might quite literally come to the boil in our descendants' lifetimes unless we act.

That's the level at which Jeremy works, and it makes him one of British poetry's best kept secrets. There was apparently a Selected Poems 1991-2004 from Troubadour Publishing in 2006 – *Lighting Up Time* – but I hadn't even realised this until I began to write this tribute, and if I wanted a copy now it'd cost me (currently) £99.35, albeit with free delivery, via Amazon. This suggests that a Collected – not necessarily a Complete Poems, but a generous overview of 300 or so pages – is long overdue, ideally in hardback, as it might only be possible to measure the scope of Jeremy's achievement in the context of such a collection. Is there a publisher out there who is willing to take up the challenge?

CHRISTINE KOUTELIERI Alternative Ways of Being

I like that about birds,
that quivering anxiety,
the way they're always tense,
tuned up, instinct
signalling the worst –

their insubstantial beings,
the hollowness of their bones,
the absence of flesh;
sight, perception, action
powered by blood and air,
the gleaming, blackberry eye,
every fine feather edged up,
ready to take flight,
to let go of earth.

PATRICIA LEIGHTON Old Man of High Wood

small   fenced off   too up and down
for the farmer's plough   timber's profit
just landmark now

one small track   north to south
is all that remains of the tread
of men's feet

the rest long forgotten   a tangle
of wild impassable undergrowth
thorns and roots

i am its guardian   chronicler   bard
shift through its layers of shadows
leave no mark

i am soil made man   gnarled as bark
tendrilled   twisted   voiceless
always here

some nights I drift to its heights   gaze down
over meadows   homesteads   bathed by
clear skies

i haunt the track's edges   merge into trees by
the boundary's barbed gate   look for lights
ascending

but no one comes
no one comes

PATRICIA LEIGHTON The Alternative Guide to Worcester Cathedral

(Happy memories, Jeremy!)

Floor plans to hand visitors gaze round   admire the vastness of space   the soaring splendour of vaulted ceilings   the play of colours from stained glass   a cool abundance of stone and marble.

If they catch a whiff of horse dung and leather   a clatter of restless hooves   the tread of troopers' boots   no one comments   echoes and ancient smells   are par for the course in a place like this

                    ... as are the cathedral's residents.

Sensing the familiar   the bored Viking oozes from his scraps of flayed skin   floats from his library prison along a cloister   walk to the nave   wonders if Cromwell might be taking on mercenaries

while a pale-faced Prince Arthur   furious with his father for landing him in yet another god-forsaken place instead of London peeps from the tracery of his chantry   asks if they'd consider a retrospective regicide.

King John   still in a miff about his lost jewels and the humiliation of Magna Carta   yells up from his chancel tomb *get over yourself lad – if it's good enough for me ...*

Pilgrim Sutton   ex-town bailiff   wakes   drags his old bones from beneath a slab   clanks down to the crypt to sigh over the remains of his knee-length boots and staff   creeps back to dream.

Clusters of monks wait until windows darken   doors are closed then with whoops and a whirl of habits make merry hell   deflower the best efforts of the Ladies of the Flower Guild   run spectral fingers over organ keys

play kiss and chase between rows of chairs   all but Brother Ambrose who   chastised for shoddy penmanship in the scriptorium sulks against a pillar   stabs at a hymn book's pages with a spare quill curses his tormentor   throws it to the floor and slowly tag ends the conga back to holy graves.

Keys turn and the cathedral opens to a new day   a duty steward checks brochures   prepares smiles   tuts as a verger (hung over after a boozy night at The Farrier's Arms) mopes in late   begins his customary check of nave and aisles   picks up the abandoned hymn book   examines the damaged pages and swears . . .

bloody mice   at it again!

RUPERT M LOYDELL King of the Mind

Without their writer's approval, words
are homeless on the page beside me,

diverse work shaped by alternative forms
battling on the boundary between experiment

and purpose. It is fascinating to require our
own irregular absence, pay attention instead

to overheard questions, various members of
the blues universe who've been reinterpreting

earthquakes all afternoon, serenading the moon
and ensuring a short steady rumble of music

beneath my delusions and dreams, a constantly
fluid, endlessly variable, deluge of good vibes.

PHIL MAILLARD Easter Monday, Válor to Nechite Valleys

A white cloud
    slides down the valley;
        blue behind it.
A sun & cloud afternoon,
        not warm,
    not cold.
The upper path
    between the valleys is
        a degree wilder
    than the lower slopes:
tumbled stone walls,
    optimistic plantings
        of olive & almond;
a tractor and harrow
    by the track. Otherwise,
        puddles, boar prints, hillsides
of encina oak & scrub & stone;
    beehives; dead black
        twisted trunks; the cry
of a buzzard, and 4 eagles
        romping in the updraft
    then turning south.
Distant dogs barking;
        goat bells; yellow lichen
on tilted boulder slabs
    where we sit to rest:
        a view from masted Lújar east
along the Contraviesa
        to four-square Gádor,

flat top in cloud.
      And resting with us
   spread out over
some dried-out lavender,
    a Scarce Swallowtail –
       new from chrysalis?
   It stays motionless
for a good twenty minutes,
    black stripes on
the palest yellow, flat
     against the bush,
ignoring us; and then
   gone.

Sierra Nevada, Andalusia, 2019.

CHRIS McCABE *fearfirefree*

DAVID MILLER Isn't or is

is or
isn't

my teeth
crunch

into a
sweet-

meat

& its tiny
tin foil tray

silver
but un-

obtrusive

– this provided
by two poets

we're visit-
ing

& I
spit out

& my wife then
knows better

(thus:
twists

& turns

in & out
of definition

& grammar)

Note: This was written after a visit with Jeremy Hilton and the late Kim Taplin at their home in Bridport.

ESTER MUCHAWSKY-SCHNAPPER Hackney, 2004

The courtyard of the hospital
seen from up through a window
late, after midnight, all alone
hard electric lights on an empty prison yard.
And I pray to You
and You don't answer
I pray to You
and You don't show
I pray to You
convinced You are there
praying words I hardly understand
but You do.
And all the while the baby struggles
closed into an unyielding womb
and then, in early daylight
the baby is born
fresh and round
and You knew

ESTER MUCHAWSKY-SCHNAPPER — Early Morning in Talbyieh and Berlin

A whiff of distant memory
humid fields, brown earth and
tall black trees
present and beloved
a childhood in Berlin.

A moment's flash-back
buried for so long
to which no delight nor effort
will let me hold on
'cause very soon
it will be gone.

A first bird's call intrudes the sudden image
an airplane crossing the silent sky
another bird's high-pitched voice cuts through
the blue-still end of the night
while a cat starts rumbling in the garbage bin.

And more birds chatter
into the night's space
a stage all to themselves
till motor-sounds push their voices aside
and …
Berlin is gone.

Brought by the night's final breeze
through an open window to a mysterious sky
a glimpse to long-past happiness
thought lost
but strangely still alive.

JOHN MUCKLE Mystery Caps

A folded screen-door shut against the wind
Dad laying a carpet beside the sea
Old floorboards inches above the sand
Something we picked up there, washed up
Man-made, scattered on the planks
Bottle tops of a rare red starry design
Picked up, treasured, jewels studding kelp
Grandad said would be worth collecting
Dad's on his knees in the far corner
Against a clock the last tack tickled into place
I seem now to feel those waves again
The slanted horizon raced away.

JOHN MUCKLE The Watchet Miltons

On holiday you drove the car, the only car
In Watchet, around that place, a town built
Along a harbour where my grandfather, fishing
For conger eels, almost drowned one night.
When Cliff's boat capsized in toothy water.

Cliff's brother heaved coal in the paper mill
All day long, feeding the great big boiler
Which we watched being hauled away
On a flat articulated truck on YouTube,
It was the self-same one being scrapped finally.

Paper with raw timber from Quantock Hills
They made back in the seventeenth century
Compressing wood-pulp in a small cider press.
You raced the family dog against Cliff's greyhound
Across those hills & his heart near stopped.

Circling around we looked out for a name
& there it was, right there on a minicab firm,
Other descendants, cousins of my cousins,
People I never knew, great chains of tangled being
& others still, from way across the Severn.

Harold Hare's cape & white mittens pressed,
His pocket-watch slow by two minutes fast
Comes back with comic cuts & chips, a pasty,
That madeleine of the West Country larder
You don't mind pulling in for at the border.

HELEN NORTHFIELD Hilton Honours Torrance

The poet
reads in slow fashion

"since you went away
I have done nothing but read & write"

A tremor of hand
carries vibrato to voice
delight falling upon paper
in perpetual smile

The intimacy of years in bicycle tales
and a chorography of words

This knowledge of a brother
paints its picture

        "since you went away
          I have done nothing but read and write"

CHRIS OZZARD The Yellow Bird

If I'd spy spindle bars on a twitcher's phone
flare glass in a scroll of rares noted through-
out the length & breadth of duh Kin'dom.

By delight do switching AI binos lick sun-
light's truest prism onto a Scarlet Tanger (♀)
in a Halifax garden. A company of Hawfinch
from the Wash to the Welsh Marches bodes
November is the Patagonian Picnic Table.

O'er which clouds are bright'ning, thou dost float and run;
Like an unbodied joy whose race is just begun.

Black Scoter ganders, Northern Divers &
an Eyebrowed Thrush in North Ronaldsway.
A Longbilled Dowitcher follows Orkney's first
Brownfooted Booby as in Scilly St Mary's
where patient methody on the daily count
delivers umpteen scarcities from dawn 'til
dusk scoured by persistent sea watchers.
Click click the counters click Pied Wheatear,
Desert Wheatear, joined by the Beachy Head
Northern Wheatear all at Sleaford Head, by & by.

Things more true and deep than we mortals dream,
Or how could thy notes flow in such a crystal stream?

A potential Central Asian Lesser Whitethroat
is being determined as we speak on Barra, Outer
Hebrides then back to Aldhelm's Head more
Pallas Warblers amid Dusky Warblers there too …
A scramble to Amble for a one-day Lesser Grey Shrike,
where a Great Grey Shrike is captured on zee camera trap;
a fifth county record of the twenty-first century
at Carlton Marshes. At Garnishee Point, Co. Cork
a first wintering Red-backed Shrike. Like a litter letter
a *Stork* carton unsettles off a roof at Ambridge.

Better than all treasures that in books are found,
Thy skill to poet were, thou scorner of the ground!

Quite why are the Hawfinches stopping at the borders
of Wales? A hybrid male Mallard x-American Black Duck
is in Stinky Bay? A drake Green-winged Teal at Marsh Lane,
with a Smew or two? Why does it matter in the tatters
of a tick? ... with a late Olive-backed Pipit on Fair Isle.
This week's Suffolk tally is for four European Serin,
Richard's Pipit, five Hoopoes, two Red-breasted flycatchers,
a Black Kite, two Rosy Starlings and a continuing Greater
Short-toed Lark, and a showy, yellow-faced Shore Lark
in six counties' records. Another popular addition concerned
the tame Lapland Bunting at Staines Reservoir, London sidling
up to the photographers, with a "bye-bye ... " Overhead honey,
or was it a pale long-legged buzzard flew?

Such harmonious madness from my lips would (not) *flow*
The world should listen then, as I am listening now:

Coda

To these loud days of numbing everythingness, a fat
woodpigeon in the ivy cooing endlessly, the much-
reduced jackdaws, an urban herring gull waiting for a sand-
wich to drop. A pretty determined dunlin cleaning up every speck.
Then bang the woodpigeon has been dropped by a goshawk
here in my town yard, mercilessly being stripped of feather,
before the breastbone is levered apart to reach the heart
& tender victuals & lights; then that's it the headless carcass
left for weeks on top of the tin roof, visited by scores of rats.

Our sincerest laughter with some pain is fraught;
Our sweetest songs are those that tell of saddest thought.

Those many days we have walked together, are to me
now left breathless, esteemed blessings. Afeared
more than once yet settled by gentians blue; or an up-
rising snipe with Beth; or near tumbling over a Curlew.

On an early outing with Kim to Tregaron Bog in the hide,
I bereft of binos watching an otter up on its haunches
eat a whole salmon like a watermelon slice! Each slice
of my life has the ellipses of your visits (your spirited generosity)
Recently, on one of mine, an outing with Kim to the Somerset Levels –
Our tally: a Ring-tailed Harrier, the antiphonies of mating
Silverwashed Fritillaries & another special moment shared
a Bittern (my first) whose lumbered flight flew up & over us.

Rain-awaken'd flowers, all that ever was
Joyous, and clear, and fresh, thy music doth surpass.

The borrowed triolets of Shelly's *To A Skylark* have been abridged as couplets between the stanzas above ... & Bird Guide's Nov 15 twitchers tally across the UK, is fair swiped ...

ELAINE RANDELL

You always know when Jeremy is in a room, he projects a sense of safety, general calm, goodness and reliability. Never a man to push himself forward, his non-confrontational sensitivity always provides a reassurance that he is listening closely with both an acute intelligence and of note, empathy.

I have known Jeremy for over 50 years, hard to pin point a date but he has always popped up in my life at junctures and cross roads with a light wisdom that always remains with me. Jeremy and I shared a profession, both social workers working at the coal face with children and families who were inevitably challenging by the nature of their complex histories and subsequent needs. Often very difficult decisions need to be made about removing children from dangerous situations and I know that Jeremy, never a person wanting or actually able to upset anyone, found this particularly hard. Jeremy retired long before me and he has enjoyed a long fruitful retirement in North Oxfordshire with his partner Kim until her death this year. His work as a poet is hugely respected but remains largely unsung.

Jeremy, with quiet, self-effacing manner would never tell you that he is related to James Hilton, the author of 'Goodbye Mr Chips' nor that he has written Chamber music or a novel, based on his professional social work experiences.

In the 1980s, as a family, we were keen to move to Herefordshire. At the very point when my husband, Ian, found a job as the Manager of Fostering and Adoption services in Gloucestershire our home in Kent was blighted by potentially being the route for the High Speed rail link. This made our home virtually impossible to sell. I was busy working in Kent and managing three children under five years. Jeremy immediately volunteered his home to Ian and so, for six months, Ian lived with Jeremy from Monday to Friday, returning home for the weekend. Not an easy time for us as a family but Jeremy's kindness and generosity was a lifesaver.

As close friends of Chris Torrance, Jeremy and I would often speak about him, his astonishing work as a poet, gardener and brew master, his spartan lifestyle, and in later years our joint concern for Chris' ability to sustain living at Glenmersher Isaf. Chris adored Jeremy, that was evident and understandable. No one could fail to be moved by his Elegy for Chris, part of it here:

>   but there are other roads
>
>   more
>
>   ancient   inward   or unseen

           hidden lines
                      connecting the
great stones   higher
               up the valleys
        trackways through the forests
        and the hills
stony streambed tracks   the dipper's
          territory   raven's roads
or buzzard's
                      on corridors of air
      roads of the spirit   roads
worked into poetry
        where the spores
  linger   and the wind finds
a millisecond of quiet   eye of
        the storm
                    shadows of the
past and future
     intersections   of the soul

Jeremy Hilton, a very fine poet, man and friend.
Kent, October 2024

ANTHONY RUDOLF Jeremy Hilton

Jeremy and I overlapped at Cambridge in the early sixties but we did not meet until nearly half a century later. At the time, I read and admired his poems in student magazines. This timescape means that whenever I conjure up the world of Cambridge poets, my memory is not of a person but of a voice on the page, a poet's voice, a disembodied voice. That remains true even now: Cambridge Hilton, for me, is a phenomenon distinct from his embodied presence when we meet in the British Library or Royal Academy. As for the voice, it remains in full flow, in both verse and prose, but now it is embodied. On his 80th birthday, I celebrate not only the man, not only the poet, but the abiding memory of a voice emanating from words on the page, sixty years ago.

AIDAN SEMMENS

The name Jeremy Hilton seems to have been part of my awareness of the poetry world since the mid-1970s, but I was late coming to a proper acquaintance with the work, and still later the man. When I finally picked up a copy of *Shadow Engineering*, something like twenty years after its publication, I'd got no further than the first page before I recognised a kindred spirit, not only for the deep affection we share for the Orkney islands and their birdlife, but also for a shared sense of the rightness and the wrongness of the world. The craft and precision with which Jeremy imparted this in his writing was at once something I knew I could aim for.

In 2020, I was privileged to be able to publish the first ten poems from his wonderful sequence *Fulmar's Wing* in *Molly Bloom*, the online magazine I was running at the time, where I related it to 'that particular feeling of envy-tinged admiration when you read something you wish you had written yourself – and almost imagine you could have written, given more time, more application, and maybe more skill'. When *Fulmar's Wing* made its appearance in book form from Knives Forks & Spoons in 2022, I reviewed it for *Tears in the Fence* magazine, where the first selection from it had appeared, concluding, 'If poetry can be important (discuss), this is an important book.' I can think of no book of poetry this century that has been, and is, more important to me; a book that wraps together, vitally and viscerally, a concern for both the wild creatures of the Earth and the people who have been, and are being, made to suffer by the callousness of governments and corporations, by man's inhumanity to man, woman and child. Care, intelligence and empathy are at the heart of this writing, as they are at the core of the man.

Jeremy visited us in Orkney in 2023, cheerfully making the long drive from southern Dorset to the northern fringe of Scotland on his own in a car whose better days seemed well past. This poem, and these images, are an attempt to capture one fleeting, but indicative, moment from that visit.

AIDAN SEMMENS On Marwick Head

That crawling, wrinkled sea, flint-like
at this vertiginous angle, utters its roar
and boom in a parallel existence,
deep bass drone to the chanting pipes
of an orchestra of auks. My lens
is trained near the horizon, on alert
for the clean white flashes that signal
gannet wings turning brilliantly.

The lightest touch on my arm
and Jeremy's gesturing with a glance
to the razorbill that stands, too close
for sharp focus, by a pink tuft of thrift
at the cliff's lip, regards us a moment
with a dark eye that shines
among the black of feathers,
then steps off into the updraught.

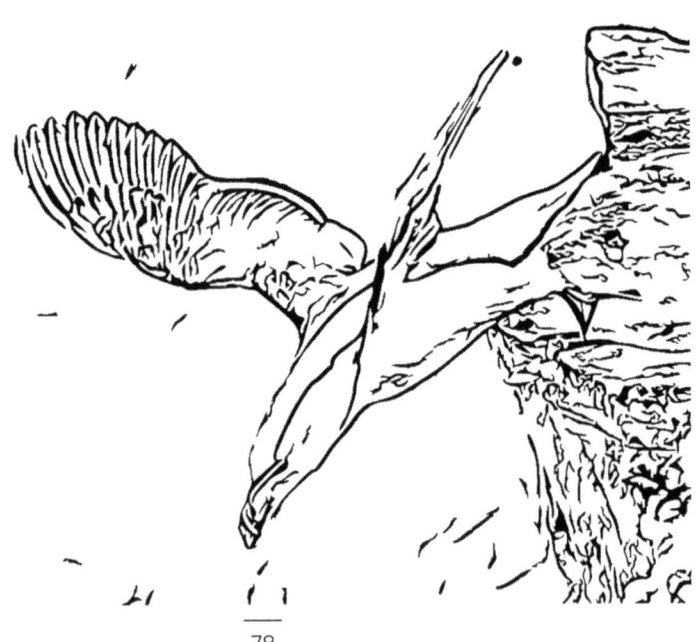

SAM SMITH Jeremy Hilton's 80th

I think I first met Jeremy – for certain: there could have been previous introductions at readings – in Paul Sutton's house. I was in Oxford for a book fair where Paul and I were to launch his first collection, *Broadsheet Asphyxia*. While Paul and Jeremy could readily be seen as poet and personality opposites, I believed that I probably came closer to Jeremy's personality, his having been a probation officer and my having been a mental health nurse, as well as my sharing with Jeremy an editor's more forgiving outlook on the poetry world. Because by that time I think Jeremy and I had both rejected and included the other's work in our respective magazines, my *Journal* and Jeremy's *Fire*.

"*Fire* magazine comes through my letterbox like a brick," Phil Knight once told me. With its red cover and thick black binding each issue of *Fire* almost had the weight of that brick. While our poetry was very different, what I think Jeremy and I had in editorial common was a desire to extend poetry's boundaries, if not in the same directions. We both, for instance, had a fondness for Paul's outspokenness even when he might, perish the thought, outspoke against either of us. The *Fire* brick was that size I think as Jeremy tried to include as many types of poetry as appealed to him. *Fire* reviews, adding to its weight, were also fair. As has been his fondness for anyone seriously attempting poetry, his own being quietly naturalistic.

There was a period when Jeremy came up to Cumbria to visit his ailing mother that he used to include a visit to us in Maryport. I don't think on those visits that we ever discussed poetry much, rather he took me to places he knew in Cumbria, sharing his love of and concern for the natural world along the way. I can recall his glee at spotting a pair of golden plovers on a Solway beach; and his deciding against going any further up one of the fells in a gale. I have a photo of him leaning into the gale. One of the reasons we didn't much mention poetry on those visits was because by that time Jeremy was more preoccupied with his composing. Music being another shared joy and passion. Happy 80th, Jeremy.

SIMON SMITH Night's Return, Dance Home

In the dead of night halfway home, giving tigers the slip,
the mountain's deep shadow, wife & kids tucked up & snug,
observe & track the Northern Dipper, low & into the river.
Venus beams all light, arching & overhead, into vast Infinity:
when cupping a hand around a candle, two tapers left, smoulder.
From across the gorge, a terrified, solitary gibbon yells out once.
Ancient & exhausted, snow for hair – I don't care – jig & chant,
Malacca cane eyeless & spaced out – *Did you see that! – All in one!*

Du Fu
Book 21, Poem 17

STEVE SPENCE Poem After Andy Brown and Andy Marvell

in a grown man
in a groan sitcom
in a great orb
in a grocer's garret
in a gibbet gander
in a gonebeforeparent
in a gizzard gazzumper
in a gold green jumper
in a green glade
in a green time
in a green goldfish
in a green garfish
in an old green jacobite
in a mould green hermaphrodite
in a manic green gluefish
in a green groaning stewdish
in a garbled green gunner
in a green green green green runner   bean
in a in a in a in a inna innergreens
in a grey green sealskins'
in a green overripe munchkins'
in green radish potatoes
in French underground daygloes
in green spinach gormless
in green gravy rope-ends
in matchless green shirtleaves
in mellifluous dry trees
in a greasy green yesterday
in underdrown green gobsmack
in a green statistic
in a blue yellow green holistic   ambulance
GREEN DOG

STEVE SPENCE Storm Cloud with Geese (after a photograph by James Ravilious)

storm CLOUD geese cloud
fade all language laughter

storm cloud GEESE cloud
freeze an aftershaven tent

storm storm a CLOUD CLOUD
clods of oaken mild minerva

CLOUD storm CLOUD storm
render all mattresses intangible

geese cloud STORM geese
render unto Caesar's halo

storm a geese goose a CLOUD
papery whites on end resin

clouds of GEESE a GEESE storm
never-ending leering ninnies

GUESS a goose cloud a CLOUD
coffin larks beneath a sky

cload a cloddin GAS goose
make it all up as he went backwards

gassin gooses STORM a cloud
waspish wonders in a dome

GHOST a goose guess STORM STORM
frighten a neighbour hear no ill

STORM cloud GEESE cloud
fade all laughter language

PAUL SURMAN Beauty

He walks along narrow paths
in the tangled daylight dark of the wood
arriving at the glade where the goddess lives
a lonely immaculate life.

The goddess sitting or the goddess lying down,
it doesn't matter which. He notes the perfection
of her flesh, her famous alabaster skin.
She turns towards him. But the alignments
of her flawless face, a symmetry
meant to be sublime, leave him indifferent.

He doesn't desire her. Like masculine gods,
her thoughts are absolute, but love only lives
in imperfections. His is a rougher wisdom.

PAUL SURMAN The Simplest Poem

Today I shall hide from the day's images.
Stay indoors to see, from the kitchen window,
rainfall like data scrolling down a screen
until, unaccounted for, it drains into the earth.
A few drops linger on the leaves of plants.

A small bird flies a low level mission. It's easier
not to get immersed, to see them, then let them go.
Not to think how artful the artless is.

Not to think how a drop of rain hanging
like an earring from the branches of a bush
contains a distorted picture of its surroundings.

How looking at things moves from seeing
to reverence to words that seek them out,
to explain the little that needs to be explained.

PAUL SURMAN Size

I've never seen the Grand Canyon.
I don't want to. It's only a hole in the ground.
Too Showy, and far too obvious.

I'd rather sit in a Chiltern's woodland –
the trees casting a modest communal shade –
and watch the sun crash soundlessly through them
on a beam that lands on the fronds of a fern,
and is so attentive it's as if it's examining its fractals.

The only other onlooker
is the stealth that's always picking its way
from tree to tree. Nobody sees it,
but everyone feels it's there, just behind them.
The ghost we don't believe in,
that has no size or shape, but won't go away.

MICHAEL W THOMAS Killay, Gower Peninsula

Two horses in a drop-away field
on the last Friday in August.

The afternoon wants to be done with itself.
On the road below, the burr of departing luggage

begins to tail off. The field is dotted
with blows of marram grass, seeded by lost winds.

On the gate are sacks for feed, empty now,
as if slipped from the shoulders of postmen

in another, wordless time. The horses shift ground.
They could still be hefting the longest day.

Done with traces, they are, with shepherding
barge-flanks, standing off as barrels tumble into hell ...

no fair-day finds them now, no small uncertain hand
curries the air they displace. Peace is a decline in scrubby green.

Lights come on in houses. The lane beside the field
stows its trees. A single bird sings down the hour.

This is the world abating itself as in a rear-view mirror.
Soon even the lairiest fly will vanish underleaf ...

soon there will be daubs only, hints of mane, eyes in soft orbit –
a canvas that, tired of gilt and riot, gingerly unpaints.

MICHAEL W THOMAS Hallow Waters

It's time to walk around the silent lake
as far as the copse that lost its tenderest children
in the last of the autumn storms,
then double back. The year hunches forward,
seeing and not seeing the space between its knees.
So too does the world, done at last
with the day's dole of cat's cradles,
sputtering oddments. Now a single wren
sings the song of time high in a stripling,
teaching its voice to a whorl of cloud
that soon enough will birth another moon,
fearful, hardly bearing to look.

Across far fields an engine revs and cuts.
A thicket speaks thorns for a moment
as something arches to pounce.
In a rowan near the water's edge,
an owl turns its head through all the hours gone,
preparing again to own what was, is and will be.
Ripples trade in whispers what the months
have gifted them: last words of final meetings,
the snap of an angler's Tupper-box,
warnings from a man who for the first time
truly knows he's a parent. The silent sigh of a woman
who threw something clear to the middle of the lake,
watched it sink,
turned her back on all of her life to that second,
then walked her emptiness along the track
till she was nothing only a twist of wind
beyond the copse with its jagged pleas,
its springtimes adjourned.

SCOTT THURSTON For Jeremy at 80

That cry-out haunts the engineer's
shadow across seven continents.
A poethics of attentive witnessing
in hope of that metaReality,
spirit beyond faith in the darkness –
words that are no single perception
even of a fulmar in flight.

Where we never found it in the looking
to sing our own song, trying to be
ourselves again in the endless longing
for light. Yes to bravely, modestly name it
love, and to act in accordance with wild
emerging visions and no limits –
turning furiously, *legato sempre.*

CHRIS TORRANCE 2 Pages From 'PATH'

1.

      dusty snows
         savour the mountain
the flock grows
ever more petulant
a cargo cult fixated
on passing land rovers

kites circle
          distinctive rake
of wings & body
          constant presenting
of angles

      red kite
colour of dark flesh

red flesh feathers
carrion eaters

      beauty in the sky
      ruby delights

          powered by
              decay &
                    death

2.

       this buzzard
       flew straight
       at me
       quite   slowly

       we were
       face-to-face
       reading each
       others thoughts
       eye-to-eye
       almost
             until

    flew about
           2 metres
      over my head

when young buzzards get heaved overboard
it is as if they dont have an identity
& that they have to
        cry themselves into an existence

CAROL WATTS Peregrine Over Blackheath

Sometimes the memory of a bird
      catches at air, a snag in atmospheres
stitched to absent skies, or that sound
      of calling in high summer now
remembered, a dark rind over the heath,
      as if matter arrives afterwards,
stumping up without migration, that you
      might know a peregrine flies here
and can retain it while you live, in these
      bright halides of your living, when
on this day so much later, the slender
      disappearance of a curlew is recorded,
its lost imprint from years of uncertainty:
      the shape of a thin scythe, silence.

JOHN WELCH Flight

(For Jeremy, Bird Watcher)

Language the contract
Between self and nothing
When bending to earth it
Exchanges the sky for words

Out walking on that
Uncertain estuary border
Where we found the beached conger –
It was starting to swell

While gull-flight lifted over
Ocean   pectoral surge –
I walked there a neighbour
To that small ancient heart

Tracing the shallow architecture
Text an invisible lintel
Being lifted into air, then how it
Breathed itself away
Reached home my mouth
Turned inside out
Radiant shadow
Fabric starfish.

JOHN WELCH Swan and Heron

This creature came round
In its purposeful circle
Charging through the air

Here just at the edge of the city
These wings were what I looked for
And how they light up the sky

Heron, neck slender and dark
As a letter turning its serif beak
Into the low October sun.

It is leaning so far forward now
Intent into the shining
Water of promise

Such fixity that gathers
All the kinds of stillness
Single-thoughted at the end of day.

CHARLES WILKINSON Jeremy Hilton's Metronome – stargazing with both feet on the ground

I first became aware of Jeremy Hilton's work during the 1970s. Fearnside's, a shop in Great Malvern that sold artists' materials, also stocked a selection of small press publications and little magazines, some of which, cyclostyled and insecurely held together by staples (or so my fallible memory insists), were in danger of falling apart if read. A slim book, perfect bound but not much longer than a pamphlet, attracted my attention, mainly because its production values were superior to most of what else was on offer. I parted with 50p and purchased *Metronome* by Jeremy Hilton (Arc, 1974).

Revisiting this work, I'm struck, as I was then, by the freshness and exactitude of the writing: an imagistic allure that feels newly minted, but supported by the gift of an acute sensitivity to the music of the line. Although a lower case first person puts in an occasional, tentative appearance, the poems are far from a parade of personality; passion, when evident, is admirably controlled, the overall effect being of the presence of emotion that never lapses into hysteria or makes unwarranted claims on the reader. In this, it seems to me, Hilton avoids the worst excesses of the Beats and the confessional school of poetry.

In some respects, it is appropriate that I found *Metronome* in an art shop, for Hilton indubitably has a heightened visual sense:

>quicksilver drizzle that fills
>the snail-slimed flowerpots

>('february')

as well as:

>timber moon wanes whiter
>   creeps towards
>dawn, dusk reddens
>   like ashy bonfires

>('an ecstasy of aloneness is a rare condition')

Whilst there's a cogent argument for saying that Hilton is a highly individual poet, who has eschewed cliques and remained unaligned to any particular group, I don't think it's mistaken to view his work in the context of the British Poetry Revival of the 1960s and '70s.

Chris Torrance is one of the dedicatees of *Metronome;* Jeremy Hilton was also, when living in Worcestershire, a good friend of the poet-physician Gael Turnbull, who whilst practising as a G.P. also added publishing, Morris Dancing and kinetic art to his accomplishments. Although of Scottish nationality, Turnbull studied, like William Carlos Williams, at the University of Pennsylvania. On returning to the U.K., he founded the magazine *Migrant,* assisted by his co-editor Michael Shayer, and subsequently the Migrant Press, which did much as a publisher and distributor, to bring the output of American poets such as Edward Dorn, Robert Creeley and Cid Corman to a British public. Turnbull also printed British poets working within the experimental/innovative tradition, including Edwin Morgan, Ian Hamilton Finlay and Roy Fisher. The press carried a flag for at least some of the poetic procedures of the American objectivists and the writers associated with Black Mountain College, where Charles Olson was one of the presiding sprits and the Rector.

Although the influence of the American strain can sometimes be detected in Hilton's use of 'white space', preference for the lower case and concise diction, his sensibility remains, in some, respects quintessentially British in its vigilant observation of his native country's landscape and seasons. In *Metronome,* there is also an alertness to the passing of time – each poem's date is listed at the foot of the page; moreover, the months ('february' 'snow in march') as well as the critical turning points in the calendar (the 'vernal equinox' and the 'summer solstice') are referenced in the titles. Although the ordering of the poems is not precisely sequential in the terms of the dates of composition, there's a strong sense of the turning seasons, supported by accurate evocations of changes in the natural world.

A striking aspect of this work is the seamless juxtaposition of the minutiae of life – not only its 'metronomic' cycle on *terra firma* – and the enormity of cosmic space:

> the first man plods,
>   with care, the
> other treads the same footprints
>   it's the safest way
>
> (music)

and in the same poem: 'multitudinous winter constellations'. There is an awareness of distance, both interstellar and terrestrial, as well as the metaphorical or actual linkage of cause and effect: 'small stone quarries with dents as though / tiny meteor fragments had cratered there' (february). The teasing out of the bond between a specific natural phenomenon with its origin continues in 'snowfall in march': the *tall streaks of sun* on a tree trunk brought in by horizontal *easterlies blizzarding.*

What is most remarkable about *Metronome* is the totality of Hilton's vision, the 'stargazing' balanced by a scrupulous attention to the quotidian as well as the capacity to strike a more intimate tone:

> I survive & write
>   I write & survive
>
> ('there is no instance that was not love')

The collection ends powerfully with a poem prompted by the partial eclipse of the moon in June 1974, which elucidates the significance of the cover, with its lunar image and swirl of constellations emphasising both the relative proximity of the earth's satellite and the vastness of outer space.

Recently, Hilton has received much merited attention in the alternative press for his substantial sequence of irregular sonnets *Fulmar's Wing* (Knives, Forks and Spoons). Yet for reasons that I'm unable to comprehend, Hilton's poetic career has, to some extent, flown under the radar as far as the mainstream is concerned. Perhaps the publication of Fulmar's Wing will bring Hilton's work to a wider public and mark his *'Briggflats* moment'. The allusion to Basil Bunting, another poet at first not given his due, seems apposite.

On a more personal note, after the publication of my first collection, I abandoned poetry for fiction for just under twenty-five years. As the indefatigable editor of the hospitable, eclectic Fire, which was far from being a 'little magazine' in terms of size and ambition, Jeremy's encouragement and generosity is warmly remembered by many writers. Jeremy was one of the first to publish me when I returned to poetry. I very much enjoyed the work by the other contributors, many of whom became friends when I once again started attending readings and festivals. It was at one such event that I first met Jeremy. He was kind enough to sign my copy of *Metronome,* which I purchased at some point in 1975/76 – and to add the date: 7th June, 2014.

MERRYN WILLIAMS Dark Glasses of Memory

The white daisies turn purple as I look back
into the dark, tunnel deeper below the surface.
I've been there before, an unhappy stranger,
frittering away the 'best years of my life'.

The students and schoolboys stream out, wan faces over uniforms
and pale anorexic girls from hours hunched at their desks.
Coughing all night, they see illumined letters spin through darkness
as on computer screens.

I go back to that time in dreams, forsaking husband and children,
wander in and outdoors to avoid my vacant room.
Those streets lie in glaring sun or methane darkness,
the last twenty-five years have been blacked out.

Back to the sixties before light changed all the colours.
There they are, the innocent-looking young, in their best years.
Their flower-like faces as they swear undying loyalty;
small, deep cracks in their emerald.

CLIVE WILMER Jeremy Hilton at Cambridge

I met Jeremy sixty years ago when we were both undergraduates at Cambridge, he at Christ's, I at King's. I don't remember our first meeting; it was probably at a poetry workshop we both attended, but there could have been other occasions. There were several promising writers around, but in that year (his second, my first) he was much the most talented.

We were writing in quite different traditions. Mine was more mainstream and British, I suppose. Jeremy was already deep into the American avant-garde. He was knowledgeable about William Carlos Williams and did more than anyone to introduce me to Williams and help me to appreciate his greatness. He also told me about Charles Olson and Black Mountain and, on this side of the ocean, Basil Bunting. I doubt if he learned much from me but he was very encouraging about my poetry, and I think he was right to claim, as he did and does, that we had something in common.

During that first year, I inherited the editorship of a little magazine that was run by King's students. To the amusement of anyone I tell about it now, it was called *Pawn* – I was too naïve to notice the possible pun and my editorship was perfectly respectable! Anyway, what I most enjoyed about the job was working out an order for the poems I had chosen, in effect comparing and contrasting them, juxtaposing the different traditions that informed them. In the issue published in November 1965, one of Jeremy's poems – a good one, I still think, and consistent with what he has written since – was printed alongside one of mine. They give a good idea of what I shared with Jeremy, as well as the obvious differences between us.

Happy birthday, Jeremy!

CLIVE WILMER Monoliths

Dateless, across distances, their stone solitude
Draws me. Moving from roads and railways
I have pressed through wooded darknesses, climbing
To gnarling crags and eroded hillcrests; and gazing
Down, I have hailed them centred in valleys,
Once more conscious of my blood.

I have slept nights
In tussocks of dewy grass flourishing
At their feet. And I have dreamt them, luminous with bird-lime,
Towering to the stars. Or lying awake, I have watched them
Watching me, their dripping bodies glistening
Silver in the moonlight.

Mellowed by the sunrise
The form is shaped. Cloaked by its dawned
Shadow, I wake and read there
The gravings of time and weather
Which speak like epitaphs. Blowing around
That tranquil indifference, a soft breeze.

In the pale morning tinged with birdsong,
I rise, and the mysterious immanence
Defines its edge, moving me beyond
Feeling. Turning, I feel my mind
Turning on that bare presence,
The still, tall centre of my wandering.

Ancient as the night they are eternally
Young as the dawn. Returning to cities
I have felt them bodying forth a past that signposts
A future, reminding me, reminding me. As echoes
Confirm the presence behind a voice, so these
Answer me.

JEREMY HILTON cairns

I have followed cairns like a lover
             (they moved me
empty of my future)

                 rain has drummed
all the hours among hours
until
                 everything else for
the senses was thieved out
                 from the sky
or from the world equally steel

they left the lump of mountain
                     bitten against
the rain
                 and the valley
snaked its mushy grey
                 among
the green sheep (moor
creatures had gone
                 under the poor world

                 feeling then
is utter) flinty as those
                 cairns
which even among those many marshed
hours
                 sold me to passion

I have often longer to go always on
following the cairns like a lover
                 (they moved me
empty of my future)

www.ingramcontent.com/pod-product-compliance
Lightning Source LLC
Chambersburg PA
CBHW042337040426
42446CB00021B/3477